# Your Dog's Lifetime Horoscope

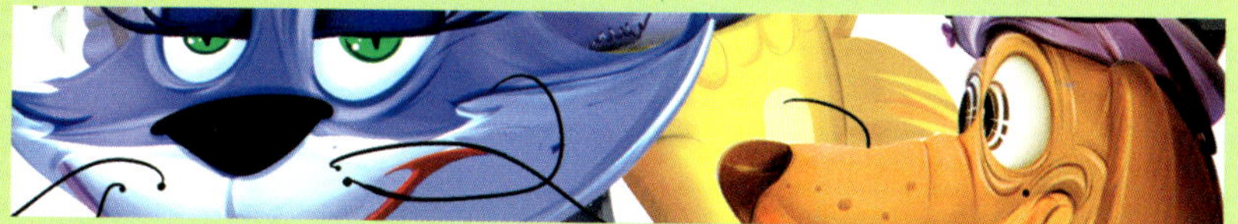

Images taken from KozmoPets™ series by L. Matusovsky

"The best thing about a man is his dog."

–French proverb

# Contents


| | | |
|---|---|---|
| **About the book** | | **4** |
| **Introduction** | | **5** |
| **Aquarius** | January 21 through February 19 | **6** |
| **Pisces** | February 20 through March 20 | **8** |
| **Aries** | March 21 through April 20 | **10** |
| **Taurus** | April 21 through May 21 | **12** |
| **Gemini** | May 22 through June 21 | **14** |
| **Cancer** | June 22 through July 23 | **16** |
| **Leo** | July 24 through August 23 | **18** |
| **Virgo** | August 24 through September 23 | **20** |
| **Libra** | September 24 through October 23 | **22** |
| **Scorpio** | October 24 through November 22 | **24** |
| **Sagittarius** | November 23 through December 21 | **26** |
| **Capricorn** | December 22 through January 20 | **28** |
| How toChoose a Name or Nickname for Your Dog the Zodiac Way | | **30** |
| How to Know the Best Time to Walk Your Dog (Without Asking the Dog) | | **32** |

# About the book

Your Dog's Lifetime horoscope is one of the few publications of its kind to explain the use of astrology in understanding the lives and fates of animals. You'll find new ways to relate to your pet as you unlock the door to your dog's real astro personality and develop perfect harmony with your treasured canine friend. This innovative work provides you with a sun-sign map to your dog's motivations and desires. You'll find useful information for choosing the best mate for your dog, for selecting a pet that will live in astrological harmony with other household pets, for picking the right name according to your kitten or puppy's Zodiac sign – even for determining the best time to walk your dog. Your Dog's Lifetime Horoscope provides new information and insight for every dog lover who wants to achieve greater communication with these ideal companions.

This is a 'must have' book for you and your best friend. Everything found in Your Dog's lifetime horoscope – based on the best astrological practices – is designed to reveal the inner life and true dog personality to both new and long-time pet lovers. With this book, you can use your pet's sun-sign to:

- Find the perfect match for you and your lifestyle using the highly detailed astrological information inside.
- Choose the best name for your pet with a never-before seen astrological formula.
- Decide on the best walking schedule with simple and unique instructions.
- Document the arrival – make your dog an official member of your family with a never-before seen Zodiac Birth Certificate.

# Introduction

This book explains how astrology works in the lives of animals. If you are a dog lover, you probably want to learn all you can about dog behavior and dogs' relationships with humans. This supplies answers to many of your questions while elucidating the undercurrents of dogs' instinctive behavior.

Just as people's horoscopes are cast regardless of race or nationality, we do not consider breed when casting dogs' horoscopes. Rather, we are concerned with the astral influence of your dog's sun sign. If you do not know when your dog was born, you should consider the time of appearance in your home as his or her birth month. For your pet, this time is truly a second birth.

I describe the compatibility between the signs of the Zodiac to help you choose the best dog for you. This tool also serves as an excellent guide for dog breeders.

If you have a dog at home, you are already a happy person. If you have problems with your pet, just open our horoscope, find the dog's sun sign and you'll be on your way to making those problems vanish. Don't have a dog yet? Your Dog's Lifetime Horoscope will help you make the perfect choice.

Luba Matusovsky

# Aquarius Dog

**January 21-February 19**

*Symbol: The Water Carrier.*
*Aquarius – an Air Sign – belongs to the element which links all living beings – the life force that flows from the atmosphere through our bodies, and out into the atmosphere again.*
***Key Words:** Friendship, Eccentricity, Freedom.*
***Dominant Principle:** "I know"*
***Ruling Planet:** Saturn*
***Stones:** Light Sapphire, Opal, Amethyst, Garnet*
***Metal:** Tin*
***Lucky Days:** Wednesday, Saturday*
***Unlucky Day:** Sunday*

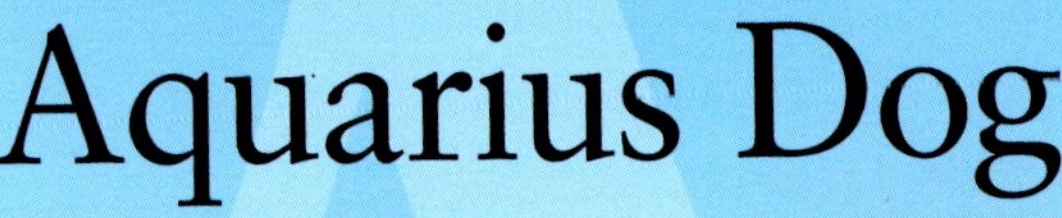

# *When you are in need, your Aquarius dog will feel and understand you without words*

Bright, eccentric, and often very funny, Aquarius Dog shines a light in any household he joins. He may exhibit some strange behavior – for instance, preferring a bizarre toy or an unusual person – but Aquarius Dog is smart and personable. He gets along easily with other pets in the household and is very kind to children. Aquarius Dog brings unfailing affection into your home. He might greet your neighbors just as loudly as he greets you, but it does not mean he likes them as much.

By nature Aquarius concerns itself with group interests. Aquarius Dog often ignores self-gratification in favor of the collective good. Aquarius's connection with humanitarian purposes makes your Aquarius Dog a great help in rescue parties and expeditions. He is perfectly suited, in fact, for any work with a good cause.

While not very demonstrative, Aquarius Dog is every bit as devoted a pet as you could hope for. When you are in need, he understands you without words. He will never leave you in the lurch, no matter how dangerous the situation. However, your Aquarius Dog doesn't make regular shows of affection. Instead he adopts a reserved or impersonal manner. This protects his personal independence and freedom.

Aquarius Dog comes to you when you are lonely or needing friendship. In some mysterious way, Aquarius Dog lifts your spirits. If the cause of your loneliness is a broken friendship, the dog may help patch things up. He may also compensate for protection that you have enjoyed in the past but are currently lacking. Whatever your circumstances, rest assured that Aquarius Dog has entered your life for a good reason.

**Compatibility with other signs:**

**Harmony:** Gemini, Libra
**Friendship:** Aries, Sagittarius
**Conflict:** Taurus, Leo, Scorpio
**Health Tips:** Although generally healthy, Aquarius Dog does not endure hot weather well. Be sure he gets plenty of vitamins and fresh air. He is susceptible to sprained knees and circulatory or cardiac disorders. He may also suffer injury when traveling or moving.

**Special Advice:** Aquarius Dog is very creative and eager to learn. He might surprise you by demonstrating tricks you never taught him. He loves to impress other dogs with his stylish appearance. Don't scold him – this is just his way of showing how different and unique he is. He might feel depressed when deprived of companionship, whether human or animal. Aquarius is blessed with an inquisitive mind and is not afraid of technology. He may even program your remote control for you!

# Pisces Dog

**February 20-March 20**

***Symbol:*** *Two fish joined together but pulling in opposite directions, exemplifying Pisces' dual and vacillating nature.*
***Key Words:*** *Sensitive, Indecisive, Compassionate*
***Dominant Principle:*** *"I believe"*
*Ruling Planet: Jupiter*
***Stones:*** *Sapphire, Moonstone*
***Metal:*** *Zinc*
***Lucky Days:*** *Monday, Thursday, Friday*
***Unlucky Day:*** *Wednesday*

# *If you want to have a lie detector of friends and foes, get yourself a Pisces dog*

Sensitive and intuitive, Pisces Dog has a special gift for distinguishing friends from foes. It's easy to mistake your Pisces pet's warnings for bad behavior, but if your normally docile dog growls at a guest, pay attention. Pisces Dog is like a walking, barking lie detector. Your human friend may turn out to be not so friendly, after all.

Pisces rules the subconscious mind. As a result, Pisces Dog is quite at home on the subconscious plane. He easily accesses human moods and dispositions, and can even sense forthcoming events. Be attentive to all your dog's signs and signals.

Pisces Dog is at his most happy and cooperative in a peaceful home environment. The Pisces symbol – two fish swimming in opposite directions but connected with a thread – expresses this love of harmony. While the thread remains strong – meaning that the harmony between you and your Pisces Dog is not disrupted – the dog can endure any hardship. Avoid upsetting Pisces Dog. Although he has a moody streak, he is staunch and collected in combat. It's hard to win against an angry Pisces.

Despite his tough side, Pisces Dog can be a real consolation to people in hospitals, meditation retreats, or any other place of voluntary or involuntary confinement. His very presence uplifts sunken spirits. He appears in your life during times of loneliness, depression, dwelling on past mistakes, or when your mind is bubbling with conflict and sorrow. Pisces Dog, with his soothing presence and keen intuition, will help you put things right. If there is discord and anger in the family, he will act as a perfect peacemaker.

**Compatibility with other signs:**

**Harmony:** Cancer, Scorpio
**Friendship:** Taurus, Capricorn
**Conflict:** Gemini, Virgo, Sagittarius
**Health Tips:** Pisces Dog has delicate health, and is quite susceptible to illness. He is also vulnerable to foot troubles and abdominal disorders. The best climate for Pisces is a dry one; avoid damp living conditions. Open mountain surroundings are especially good.

**Special Advice:** Artistic and refined by nature, Pisces Dog has a strong aversion to unrefined speech. This dog also has a special flair for the theatrical, and loves to perform! Don't be surprised if your Pisces pet takes Hollywood by storm.

# Aries Dog

**March 21-April 20**

***Symbol:*** *The Ram. Aries Dog is an aggressive leader, always ready to accept a challenge.*
***Key Words:*** *Enthusiasm, Pluck, Aggression*
***Dominant Principle:*** *"I am"*
***Ruling Planets:*** *Mars, Sun*
***Stones:*** *Diamond, Ruby, Amethyst*
***Metals:*** *Iron, Steel*
***Lucky Days:*** *Tuesday, Sunday*
***Unlucky Days:*** *Friday, Saturday*

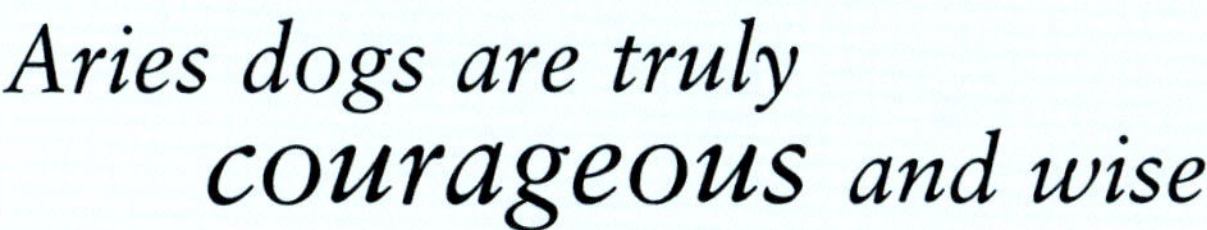

# *Aries dogs are truly courageous and wise*

Valiant, simple-hearted Aries makes an excellent guard dog. He can be aggressive – even fierce – particularly toward people who hide their evil intentions behind a smile. Aries is the first sign of the Zodiac – the starting point of life. All animals born under this sign have noble, true natures. An Aries Dog's uncomplicated heart does not mean he is dense or dull. Quite the opposite. Any Aries Dog, especially one who has survived hardship, is sure to be courageous and wise. But as with every sign, an Aries Dog can express his or her opposite nature. When oppressed, unloved, and uncared for, the Aries Dog may become selfish, over-aggressive, and unintelligent.

The Aries Dog is filled with loyalty and integrity. Cunning and guile are alien to its nature. His loyalty – however – is like a child's, and should never be slighted for any reason. If you are generous with love and praise, acknowledge all of your Aries Dog's budding achievements and he will fight tooth and nail for your honor and safety. Inspired by a positive goal, Aries is fearless.

Do you have a secret wish to enter a dog/owner look-alike competition? If so, Aries is your best bet, as these dogs often resemble their masters.

When Aries Dog appears in your house he or she heralds the death of your old bonds and commitments and the beginning of a new life. Your dog may be a providential gift, meant to supply you with courage, self-confidence, and ambition.

**Compatibility with other signs:**

**Harmony:** Leo, Sagittarius
**Friendship:** Gemini, Aquarius
**Conflict:** Cancer, Libra, Capricorn
**Health Tips:** Aries Dog's impulsive nature makes him or her prone to accidents and head injuries.
**Special Advice:** Devoted Aries Dog takes your ailments and diseases upon himself. He remains tied to you in this way as long as there is a bond of affection. Don't be surprised if your guard dog feels uncomfortable in his own doghouse, since Aries is not a fan of confinement. Highly energetic, Aries Dog gets along best with an owner who is active and outgoing.

# Taurus Dog

**April 21-May 21**

***Symbol:*** *The Bull. Like his symbol – a powerfully built, possessive animal – Taurus is unflinching in attack.*
***Key Words:*** Practicality, Possessiveness, Hedonism
***Dominant Principle:*** *"I have"*
***Ruling Planets:*** Venus, Moon
***Stones:*** *Sapphire, Agate, Turquoise, Nephrite*
***Metal:*** Copper
***Lucky Days:*** Monday, Friday
***Unlucky Day:*** Tuesday

# *Taurus dog will channel help and consolation to you*

Taurus, the sign of wealth and fertility, is also the sign of doggedness – if you'll forgive the pun – and perseverance. On the surface, Taurus Dog may appear to be a hound dog tailing his prey, but deep down he or she has more in common with a good-hearted St. Bernard.

Because he's an Earth Sign, Taurus Dog loves creature comforts – good food (particularly meat), a comfy bed, and a treasured toy. In fact, especially if untrained, Taurus Dog can be extremely lazy, even sluggish and disobedient. Train your Taurus with understanding and patience to assist his soul's evolutionary progress; otherwise he may be at the mercy of his primitive drives.

Dog breeders take note: Taurus Dog is highly fertile, with a strong sex drive. His practical, unexcitable nature also makes him well suited for pure breeding.

Taurus' place in the House of Wealth means Taurus Dog will impact your finances. He may appear in your life when you are going through a period of financial difficulties. In the realm of money, Taurus is sure to channel your help and consolation. Taurus Dog is also a good choice when purchasing a dog from a breeder: his sign's link with wealth makes him a wise investment.

**Compatibility with other signs:**

**Harmony:** Virgo, Capricorn
**Friendship:** Cancer, Pisces
**Conflict:** Leo, Scorpio, Aquarius
**Health Tips:** Taurus Dog, although usually healthy and living a long life, is, however, susceptible to throat and ear infections and obesity.
**Special Advice:** Taurus Dog always shares your emotional unrest. He will therefore do his doggy best to alleviate your problems and improve your relationships with other people. Taurus doesn't respond well to pressure and demanding people. Instead he prefers consistency and stability. Indecisive owners tend to confuse and unsettle Taurus Dog. Make good on all your promises to Taurus Dog, whether for outings, toys, or treats. If he waits too long for something he expects, he may think you have forgotten or changed your mind.

# Gemini Dog

**May 22-June 21**

***Symbol:*** *The Twins. Gemini Dog may display two very distinct personalities. This dual nature is reflected in his symbol, which resembles the Roman Numeral II.*
***Key Words:*** *Inventive, Studious, Active, Sly*
***Dominant Principle:*** *"I think"*
***Ruling Planet:*** *Mercury*
***Stones:*** *Agate, Crystal, Garnet*
***Metals:*** *Gold, Silver*
***Lucky Days:*** *Wednesday, Sunday*
***Unlucky Day:*** *Thursday*

# Gemini dogs like children and toys and *enjoy adventure* and change of pace

If you like to shake up your routine – or prefer to avoid having a routine altogether – unpredictable Gemini Dog might be your new best friend. Gemini Dog makes an excellent companion for many people. He likes children and toys, adventure and change of pace. No other dog loves traveling in the backseat of your car quite as much as Gemini does. Variety is the Gemini's motto, and Gemini Dog is no exception. He is both easily bored and tremendously talented. Gemini Dog sometimes uses his talents for less noble pursuits – such as ferreting his favorite food out of the fridge!

Despite his or her intellectual qualities and sociability, Gemini Dog is not emotionally sensitive. Because of his sign's duality, your Gemini pet changes constantly. He's sweet and affectionate one moment, a grumbly loner the next. Don't let his mood swings get to you – it's just his way.

Hunting enthusiasts take note: Geminis have a hard time as hunting dogs expected to be steadfast and persistent. So if you want your new best friend to join you in the duck blind, Gemini Dog is not your best bet.

Gemini Dog appears in your house when you miss your family, or are suffering from lack of warmth in your present environment. Friendly, energetic Gemini fills this emotional gap. Many people intuitively get a Gemini dog during lonely times, or when Gemini is activated in one's personal horoscopes.

**Compatibility with other signs:**

**Harmony:** Libra, Aquarius
**Friendship:** Leo, Aries
**Conflict:** Sagittarius, Virgo, Pisces
**Health Tips:** Gemini Dog is prone to diseases of the nervous system, exhaustion, back problems, and pulmonary disorders. Gemini Dog may suffer injury while protecting his master. He may even sacrifice his life to protect the ones he loves.

**Special Advice:** Geminis loathe monotony and repetition. Your Gemini Dog loves to be entertained. Ever notice how much he enjoys watching TV and listening to music? Don't be a bore for Gemini Dog – who likes bright, easygoing and funny people. Feel free to sing even if you do not have the voice. Your pet will love it, especially if it is a top ten hit! Indulge Gemini's thirst for excitement by bringing your canine companion along on all sorts of expeditions.

# Cancer Dog

**June 22-July 23**

***Symbol:*** *The Crab. Like the sea creature that represents him, Cancer Dog has a soft, sensitive interior and a protective exterior shell.*
***Key Words:*** *Domestic, Security, Emotional, Support*
***Dominant Principle:*** *"I feel"*
***Ruling Planet:*** *Moon*
***Stones:*** *Moonstone, Ruby, Emerald*
***Metal:*** *Silver*
***Lucky Days:*** *Monday, Thursday*
***Unlucky Days:*** *Tuesday, Saturday*

# *Cancer dogs are very devoted to their home and to their master's entire family*

Cancer, which is ruled by the Moon, has special links to the Animal Kingdom. The Moon is believed to hide Hecate, the nocturnal goddess of ghosts and mysteries. She rules the dark side of the Moon, as well as animals' instincts and the instinctive self in human beings. Thus dogs can channel these mysterious forces, often affecting the people they live with.

Cancer Dog devotes himself completely to his master's home and family. Away from the family, Cancer becomes worried and restless. For instance, a friendly, loyal Rottweiler is a typical Cancer dog. He cares deeply for family and close friends. Cancer Dog may not have many friends, but when he does find one the bond lasts forever. Cancer is likely to expresses his love and care through protectiveness. No matter who the bad guy is Cancer Dog can make him wish he'd never been born if he attacks his human friend.

Caring is what Cancers do better than anybody else. Always be kind to your Cancer Dog. He is extremely sensitive to what you say and how you talk to him. Once his feelings are hurt, Cancer Dog finds it difficult to forgive. Your hurtful words or actions will be in your dog's mind every time he sees you.

Because Cancer is associated with home and nesting, when Cancer Dog arrives in your life it may signal that a house and a family of your own are in the near future. The dog can also silently remind you of your parents and take you back to memories of your childhood and your parents' home.

**Compatibility with other signs:**

**Harmony:** Scorpio, Pisces
**Friendship:** Virgo, Taurus
**Conflict:** Capricorn, Aries, Libra
**Health Tips:** Cancer Dog has a tendency to overweight. He may also suffer from problems with his digestive tract.

**Special Advice:** Cancer Dog truly sees you, his human companion, as someone under his care. Very sensitive to the needs of elderly people and children, he intuitively knows when he's needed and never hesitates to offer help. Cancer Dog suffers anguish if his beloved family breaks up. He dislikes rude or noisy guests who intrude on the privacy of his human family. He may be injured when traveling with you.

# Leo Dog

**July 24-August 23**

***Symbol:*** *The Lion. Leo Dog takes his cues from the King of the Beasts with his power, his roar, and his regal attitude.*
***Key Words:*** *Power, Generosity, Charisma*
***Dominant Principle:*** *"I will"*
***Ruling Planet:*** *Sun*
***Stones:*** *Amber, Topaz, Emerald, Ruby, Onyx*
***Metal:*** *Gold*
***Lucky Day:*** *Sunday*
***Unlucky Day:*** *Saturday*

## *A dog born under this sign has a dignified posture and self-confidence of a royal nature*

Leo is governed by the Sun, giver of heat and light. Animals born under this sign have the dignified posture and self-confidence of royalty. Naturally lucky with their future owners, they usually join warm, loving families.

Even if your Leo Dog is not a thoroughbred, he or she will likely be choosy and jealous. But not to worry: a couple of nice words to your Leo and the lion becomes a pussycat. He rolls to one side, narrows his eyes and smiles with genuine satisfaction. (Yes, dogs can really smile!)

Every Leo knows that he is the star of the show, the center of attention, and the natural number one. Take your Leo Dog to exhibitions and dog shows galore. Like their human counterparts, Leos adore social events. What's more, Leo is a natural winner. He uses an interesting blend of selfishness and generosity to help him get ahead.

Although Leo is not as militant as Aries or Taurus, Leo Dog loves to show off and act important. He's proud not only of his master and his house, but also of his collar, his haircut, and everything that makes him conspicuous.

Though this sign is highly recommended for pure breeding, choosy Leo Dog is likely to have trouble getting himself a mate, particularly if he's a pedigree dog. It's hard for him to recognize that someone else can be as noble and dignified as him.

Leo is directly related to children and games. Leo Dog's appearance in your life may signify an absence of children. If you have children Leo Dog will play with them, and even take care of them. On the emotional level, Leo's arrival may present an opportunity for you to revive any blocked affection you may be experiencing. Leo Dog's natural sense of dignity should be respected. Whatever his or her role, Leo will always be a beautiful ornament to your home and family.

Compatibility with other signs:

Harmony: Sagittarius, Aries
Friendship: Libra, Gemini
Conflict: Scorpio, Aquarius, and Taurus
Health Tips: Leo Dog is generally very healthy, but he may experience cardiac and pulmonary troubles.

Special Advice: Your Leo Dog may cause envious or jealous reactions in other people. Leo needs appreciation, and loves it when you openly enjoy his or her company. This dog loves any form of your affection, especially presents. Your Leo Dog repays you not only with all his love and loyalty, but also with many awards and prizes from top canine competitions!

# Virgo Dog

**August 24-September 23**

*Symbol:* *The Virgin. The only feminine figure in the Zodiac, the Virgin holds an ear of wheat, which symbolizes fertility. She was worshiped as the Earth goddess throughout the ancient world.*

***Key Words:*** *Service, Practicality, Loyalty*

***Dominant Principle:*** *"I analyze"*

***Ruling Planet:*** *Mercury*

***Stones:*** *Agate, Malachite, Carnelian, Topaz, Nephrite, Yellow Sapphire*

***Metals:*** *Copper, Tin*

***Lucky Day:*** *Wednesday*

***Unlucky Days:*** *Thursday, Friday*

# *Virgo dog is extremely efficient in performing his duties*

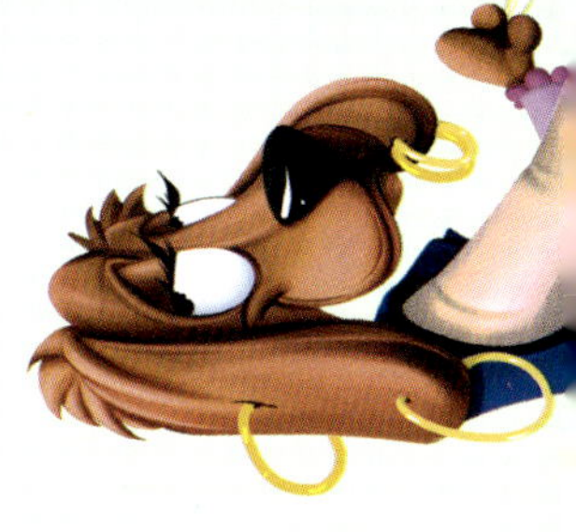

Virgo and Scorpio are the most wonderful signs of the Zodiac. Despite stereotypes that cast Virgo as the most practical sign, Virgos more often function as catalysts. Virgo connects all the signs of the Zodiac, absorbing and reflecting all of their characteristics whether positive or negative. When a Virgo is present, other Zodiac signs uncover hidden sides of themselves – pieces of their personality they'd never imagined. Because of his or her ability to cast your personality in a new light, your Virgo Dog exercises a tremendous influence on you.

Virgo Dog is the mirror that reflects all of your hidden weaknesses and strengths. In fact, he or she may provoke extremes of love and hate in family members. Some people will see him as the family's guardian angel. Others regard him as the cause of bad luck and discord. However, in both instances, Virgo Dog is no more than a reflection of people's secret faces. In this way he's actually a helper, exposing the family's hidden problems before they become serious. If peace and kindness fill your home, Virgo Dog will make it grow and flourish.

Whatever his duties, Virgo Dog is extremely efficient in performing them. He makes a great guard dog or patrol dog. A Virgo bloodhound is the best of his breed.

Since Virgo resides in the House of Health, Virgo Dog can be very sensitive to human illnesses. He may sense an ailing organ in his owner's body and lie down on it, thus taking the disease upon himself. Like humans, dogs' bodies have magnetic fields, which they can use to heal people.

Virgo Dog appears in your life when you suffer health problems or when you need a devoted helper for your work. Virgo Dog will be the first to offer a helping hand – or paw!

**Compatibility with other signs:**

**Harmony:** Capricorn, Taurus
**Friendship:** Scorpio, Cancer
**Conflict:** Sagittarius, Pisces, Gemini
**Health Tips:** Virgo Dog does not usually boast fine health. His intestines are particularly vulnerable, so pay special attention to his diet and walks. Virgo has a delicate nervous system, so avoid overloading him. Feelings of over-stimulation or being overwhelmed negatively influence the health of his whole body.

**Special Advice:** Virgo Dog is quite sensitive to unhealthy environments and to the ailments of other dogs. Thus it's important to protect him against harmful company. Invest total trust in your Virgo dog and he will protect you and your family and guard your home better than any security system.

# Libra Dog

**September 24-October 23**

***Symbol:*** *The Scales. Libra's symbol is the only inanimate object among the Zodiac signs. Libras seek in others the balancing qualities they lack in themselves. This results in their frequent indecisiveness.*
***Key Words:*** *Cooperation, Companionship, Balance*
***Dominant Principle:*** *"I balance"*
***Ruling Planet:*** *Venus*
***Stones:*** *Opal, Lazurite, Pearl, Chrysolite, Diamond*
***Lucky Days:*** *Friday, Saturday*
***Unlucky Days:*** *Tuesday, Sunday*

# *Libra dog may introduce you not only to other dogs but to their owners as well*

Libra is traditionally regarded as ruling close relationships. Many astrologers consider Libra the sign of equilibrium. But very often Libra Dog experiences periods of intense uncertainty, resulting in relationship changes and mental or emotional fluctuations. Don't get discouraged during times of instability: sooner or later, the Libra scales come to balance.

It's important to walk your canine Libra companion every day – more than once if you have the time. If you are not able to take Libra Dog out yourself, consider hiring a dog walker. Highly social, Libras need regular contact with other dogs, so take your pet to a dog park as often as possible. He or she will make plenty of friends – and even introduce you to their dog owners so that you'll have someone new to play with! Libra is ruled by Venus, the goddess of love.

Naturally quiet and peaceful, Libra Dog rarely expresses strong negative emotions. But when he does fly off the handle, watch out! An angry Libra Dog can be a real menace. One thing he will not do is bear a grudge, so rest assured that you can smooth over any misunderstandings between you and your furry Libra friend.

Libra Dog appears in your house when you need some social contact. To a certain extent, he compensates for the lack of human companionship in your life. He might also herald a forthcoming marriage or friendship. In this case, Libra Dog offers you a good opportunity to practice living in mutual harmony before you take the plunge with a human. After all, dogs are less finicky creatures than human beings.

**Compatibility with other signs:**

**Harmony:** Aquarius, Gemini
**Friendship:** Sagittarius, Leo
**Conflict:** Capricorn, Aries, Cancer
**Health Tips:** Libra dog is vulnerable to kidney disease, and may also be sluggish and have problems with his or her eyes.

**Special Advice:** A Libra dog is a dainty eater and requires a balanced diet. Because of Libra's curious nature, he or she is likely to fall into all kinds of traps. Make sure you don't accidentally shut him in your refrigerator! Libra Dog has a talent for mediating conflicts between people and will use his easy, elegant personality to release tension at home. Libra thrives in a bright and comfortable home environment. And especially loves an expensive haircut in a trendy salon!

# Scorpio Dog

**October 24-November 22**

*Symbol:* *The Scorpion and the Eagle. Together these animals rise above temptation. This sign is associated with both the life force and the life cycle.*
***Key Words:*** *Tenacity, Rebirth, Mystery*
***Dominant Principle:*** *"I desire"*
***Ruling Planets:*** *Pluto, Mars*
***Stones:*** *Ruby, Topaz, Aquamarine, Coral, Malachite*
***Metals:*** *Iron, Steel*
***Lucky Day:*** *Tuesday*
***Unlucky Days:*** *Monday, Friday*

# *Scorpio dog will form a deep and* ***lasting friendship*** *with you*

Scorpio, which represents desire, emotional struggle, and fickle fate, resides in the House of Death and Rebirth. This is a sign of enormous desire – to be, to live, to feel. Scorpio Dog expresses all these traits, but channels them through his owner rather than through himself.

Just as human fate does not depend on one person alone, an animal's fate involves other animals and people in a kind of cosmic play. This group involvement is particularly active in Scorpio Dog. Scorpios are architects of their own futures. Scorpio Dog is not content to let himself be chosen – he turns the tables and chooses you! He is a master at wiggling his way into your heart, convincing you to take him home. The dog may appear at a critical moment in your life, assisting you with personal transformation. What's certain is that once you and your Scorpio are together, the bond is unbreakable.

Never leave Scorpio Dog alone for long periods. He is prone to sudden bursts of energy – and all sorts of accidents!

Ruled by warlike Mars, Scorpio Dog is fearless and charismatic. He can sense threats and will always warn you, or even protect you, against attack.

**Compatibility with other signs:**

**Harmony:** Pisces, Cancer
**Friendship:** Capricorn, Virgo
**Conflict:** Aquarius, Taurus, Leo
**Health Tips:** Although Scorpio dog is sturdy, he may experience problems with his nose, throat, heart, back, and legs.

**Special Advice:** Scorpio Dog protects you in any situations. Very sensitive to aggressive instincts, he may have sudden angry outbursts. He can also bear a grudge. No matter what your emotions, never talk harshly to your Scorpio Dog and never force him to perform tricks for your guests if he does not want to. Scorpio Dog is an excellent tracer. He'll find that long lost sock of yours – you know, the missing half of your favorite pair – and proudly deposit it in your lap!

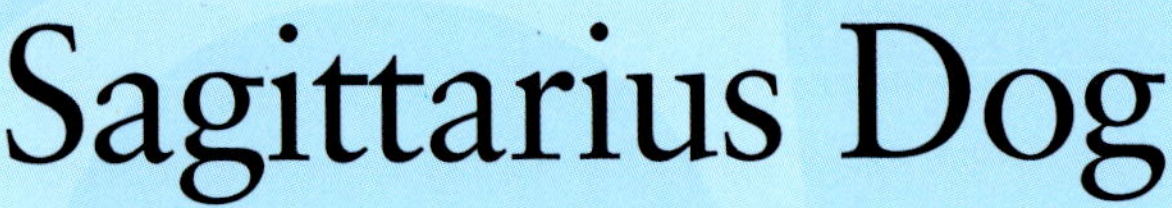

# Sagittarius Dog

**November 23-December 21**

***Symbol:*** *The Centaur with bow and arrow. Like the arrow in the Centaur's bow, Sagittarius Dog has far-reaching, free-ranging, restless, and idealistic aims.*

***Key Words:*** *Liberty, Independence, Adventure*

***Dominant Principle:*** *"I see"*

***Ruling Planet:*** *Jupiter*

***Stones:*** *Topaz, Amethyst, Sapphire, Agate, Turquoise, Carbuncle, Emerald*

***Metals:*** *Zinc, Tin*

***Lucky Day:*** *Thursday*

***Unlucky Day:*** *Wednesday*

# *Sagittarius dogs are fond of traveling with their masters*

Sagittarius embodies independence and freedom. Dogs born under this sign love liberty, adventures, and long trips. In fact, you can never truly domesticate Sagittarius Dog, so let him venture out into the world when he gets those itchy feet. You can always count on him to return. Lassie, the famous TV dog, is a typical Sagittarius. Noble and independent, she travels the country rescuing people and restoring justice.

Sagittarius Dog is never happier than when you take him on a trip. He makes an excellent hunting dog or just a nice, jolly companion for an adventure.

Expect your outgoing Sagittarius to explore the neighborhood and make other canine friends. He loves weekends and games, and he needs regular physical exercise. He will form a lasting friendship with you provided you let him enjoy his independence and freedom. Tie him down and he'll disappear without a trace.

The appearance of a Sagittarius dog in your home ushers mental or material expansion into your life. He may also be the harbinger of overseas travel, personal changes, or new experiences.

**Compatibility with other signs:**

**Harmony:** Aries, Leo
**Friendship:** Aquarius, Libra
**Conflict:** Pisces, Gemini, Virgo
**Health Tips:** Sagittarius Dog usually enjoys good health. When he does become ill, he recovers quickly. His hips and lungs are vulnerable to ailments. Don't feed your Sagittarius too many steaks as he tends to carry a little extra weight.

**Special Advice:** Sagittarius Dog is somewhat touchy, often imagining insults, so be patient with him. To make him feel better, surround him with friends. He loves good company and showing off at parties! Sagittarius is a very lucky sign for race dogs. He also does well in exhibitions and competitions. While he is a marvel of neatness and order, this adventure-loving dog is always on the move. He might just join the astronauts on a moon walk if he had the chance!

# Capricorn Dog

**December 22-January 20**

***Symbol:*** *The Goat. Capricorn is identified with various mythical "culture gods" who came from the sea (symbol of the unconscious), imparted civilization to humans, and sank back into the depths after nightfall.*

***Key Words:*** *Duty, Aspiration, Ambition*

***Dominant Principle:*** *"I use"*

***Ruling Planets:*** *Saturn, Mars*

***Stones:*** *Ruby, Onyx, Moonstone, Lazurite, Garnet*

***Metal:*** *Lead*

***Lucky Days:*** *Tuesday, Saturday*

***Unlucky Days:*** *Monday, Thursday*

# *Capricorn dog will go out of his way to incur favor from his owner*

Ambitious Capricorn takes as its symbol a mountain goat struggling to the summit – a fitting image for the sign that resides in the House of Power and Achievement. This House is likely to appear in the horoscope of Capricorn Dog's master, as well. Indeed, the life of a Capricorn dog will largely depend on his owner and his position in the owner's house.

Capricorn Dog thrives on tradition. He will protest any sudden change in relationships, roles, and household habits. When disruption occurs, especially within the family, the dog channels all his efforts into restoring the status quo. In some cases Capricorn can save a failing marriage. If you're single, you'd better sort it out with your Canine Capricorn before you bring your latest love home. A Capricorn Dog caught off guard may act hostile toward someone he sees as a strange intruder. Just assure your Capricorn that your new human friend poses no threat to his perks and rights, and everything will be fine.

Capricorn Dog makes every effort to win favor from his owner, the main symbol of power in the dog's eyes. So if you want him or her to be a guard dog or watchdog, your Capricorn will work responsibly and selflessly. If you live a secluded life and enjoy meditation, Capricorn Dog will try to please you by tuning into your wavelength. In this way he can help you achieve mental quiet. He is particularly good with this kind of help, as Capricorn Dog boasts a highly developed sense of intuition.

Capricorn Dog often appears in your life at the peak of your career. If your work is not being recognized, he will compensate by attracting attention to you. Even if your Capricorn Dog does not win the first prize at a dog show, he will make you proud of him in some other way.

Compatibility with other signs:

Harmony: Taurus, Virgo
Friendship: Pisces, Scorpio
Conflict: Aries, Cancer, and Libra
Health Tips: Capricorn Dog is usually healthy, with a tendency to skin rashes and similar disorders. He is prone to calcium deficiency, which could lead to some tooth and bone disorders. Humidity and cold have an adverse effect on Capricorn, so be sure to protect your dog from extreme weather.

Special Advice: When well loved and cared for, Capricorn Dog may incite feelings of envy in your neighborhood – especially if you live in a competitive or showy area. Capricorn Dog offers you total devotion, and he wants you to show him that he's appreciated. If you are hosting a company party at your house, Capricorn Dog picks your boss out of the crowd like magic. If your boss is a dog person, canine Capricorn is sure to befriend him or her. Let your pet warm up your boss's heart – there's no better time to ask for that raise or promotion!

## How to Choose the Best Name for Your Dog.... Without Asking Him!

Every name corresponds to a particular astrological number, which should be concordant with your and your pet's Zodiac signs.
To live in harmony with nature and to increase your pet's happiness and health, make sure you choose the right name for your furry friend by following the recommendations given below.

In astrology, each number corresponds to a certain planet. Each planet, in turn connects to a Zodiac sign. Similarly, each letter (which becomes a vibration when pronounced) corresponds to a certain number (see table below).

| 1 | 2 | 3 | 4 | 5 | 6 | 7 | 8 | 9 | 10 | 11 | 12 |
|---|---|---|---|---|---|---|---|---|---|---|---|
| A | B | C | D | E | F | G | H | I | J | K | L |
| M | N | O | P | Q | R | S | T | U | V | W | X |
| Y | Z | | | | | | | | | | |

You can use a series of fairly simple calculations based on these principles to find the numerical value of any name. If the value of a name is 10 or greater, add the digits together to find the new value. Repeat this process until you get a single-digit result. For example, if you calculate a value of 49: 4+9 =13; 1+3 =4

1 Names with a numerical value of 1 are favorable for Leo and Aries. They are in disharmony with Aquarius, Cancer, and Libra. Example: BABE = 2+1+2+5 =10; 1+0=1

2 Names with a value of 2 are favorable for Cancer or Taurus. They are in disharmony with Capricorn and Scorpio. Example: DUKE = 4+9+11+5 =29; 2+9= 11; 1+1=2

3 A value of 3 works well with Aries, Capricorn, and Scorpio but is in disharmony with Cancer and Libra. Example: BIM = 2+9+1 = 12; 1+2 =3

4 4 is in harmony with Gemini but does not work well with Pisces and Scorpio. Example: MIKA = 1+9+11+1 = 22; 2+2 =4

5 5 is good for dogs born under Virgo, Cancer, and Pisces. It is not favorable for Sagittarius and Capricorn. Example: MAX = 1+1+12=14; 1+4=5

6 6 is in harmony with Libra, Pisces, and Taurus. It is in disharmony with Aries, Scorpio, and Virgo. Example: ABBA = 1+2+2+1=6

7 7 works well with Scorpio and Libra but is in disharmony with Aries and Cancer. Example: SHADOW = 7+8+1+4+3+11 = 34; 3+4=7

8 8 is good for Aquarius and Scorpio dogs. It is not compatible with Taurus and Leo. Example: RAM = 6+1+1 = 8.

9 9 works well for Pisces, Aquarius, and Sagittarius but is in disharmony with Leo and Gemini. Example: SAM = 7+1+1 =9

**The following table will help you find your pet's favorable astrological number:**

| | In harmony (Favorable number) | In disharmony (Unfavorable number) |
|---|---|---|
| Aries | 1, 3 | 6, 7 |
| Taurus | 2, 6 | 8 |
| Gemini | 4 | 9 |
| Cancer | 2, 5 | 1, 3, 7 |
| Leo | 1 | 8, 9 |
| Virgo | 5 | 6 |
| Libra | 6, 7 | 1, 3 |
| Scorpio | 3, 7, 8 | 2, 4, 6 |
| Sagittarius | 9 | 5 |
| Capricorn | 3 | 2, 5 |
| Aquarius | 8, 9 | 1 |
| Pisces | 5, 6, 9 | 4 |

## Finding the Best Time to Walk Your Dog.... Without Asking Him!

The best times to walk your dog are the hours ruled by Mars and Sun. Each day of the week is ruled by one planet:

| | | |
|---|---|---|
| Sunday | – | Sun |
| Monday | – | Moon |
| Tuesday | – | Mars |
| Wednesday | – | Mercury |
| Thursday | – | Jupiter |
| Friday | – | Venus |
| Saturday | – | Saturn |

The planets also rule the hours of every day. The first hour following sunrise is ruled by the day's ruling planet. Therefore, on Sunday, the first hour belongs to the Sun; on Monday, to the Moon; on Tuesday, to Mars; on Wednesday, to Mercury; and so on. The planets rule each subsequent hour in a rotating sequence, re-beginning every eighth hour with the day's ruling planet. (See the table below.)

For example: On Sunday, the sequence begins with the Sun and continues with Venus, Mercury, Moon, Saturn, Jupiter, Mars, Sun, and so on. On Tuesday, while the pattern remains the same, the sequence begins with Mars – Tuesday's ruling planet – followed by Sun, Venus, Mercury, Moon, Saturn, Jupiter, Mars, Sun, etc.

After sunset, the planet sequence begins with the fifth planet after the day's ruling planet.

**(After Sunrise)**

| | 1st hour | 2nd hour | 3rd hour | 4th hour | 5th hour | 6th hour | 7th hour | 8th hour |
|---|---|---|---|---|---|---|---|---|
| SUNDAY | SUN | VENUS | MERCURY | MOON | SATURN | JUPITER | MARS | SUN |
| MONDAY | MOON | SATURN | JUPITER | MARS | SUN | VENUS | MERCURY | MOON |
| TUESDAY | MARS | SUN | VENUS | MERCURY | MOON | SATURN | JUPITER | MARS |
| WEDNESDAY | MERCURY | MOON | SATURN | JUPITER | MARS | SUN | VENUS | MERCURY |
| THURSDAY | JUPITER | MARS | SUN | VENUS | MERCURY | MOON | SATURN | JUPITER |
| FRIDAY | VENUS | MERCURY | MOON | SATURN | JUPITER | MARS | SUN | VENUS |
| SATURDAY | SATURN | JUPITER | MARS | SUN | VENUS | MERCURY | MOON | SATURN |

Then the same rotating sequence applies. For instance: On Sunday, the first hour after sunset will be Jupiter; the second – Mars; the third – Sun; and so on. (See table below.) If your count goes past midnight, it should be considered the next day and thus ignored. Remember: The best hours to walk your pet are those ruled by Mars and Sun.

**(After Sunset)**

| | 1st hour | 2nd hour | 3rd hour | 4th hour | 5th hour | 6th hour | 7th hour |
|---|---|---|---|---|---|---|---|
| SUNDAY | JUPITER | MARS | SUN | VENUS | MERCURY | MOON | SATURN |
| MONDAY | VENUS | MERCURY | MOON | SATURN | JUPITER | MARS | SUN |
| TUESDAY | SATURN | JUPITER | MARS | SUN | VENUS | MERCURY | MOON |
| WEDNESDAY | SUN | VENUS | MERCURY | MOON | SATURN | JUPITER | MARS |
| THURSDAY | MOON | SATURN | JUPITER | MARS | SUN | VENUS | MERCURY |
| FRIDAY | MARS | SUN | VENUS | MERCURY | MOON | SATURN | JUPITER |
| SATURDAY | MERCURY | MOON | SATURN | JUPITER | MARS | SUN | VENUS |

**Use these tables to quickly find the hours ruled by Mars and Sun.**

| After Sunrise: | |
|---|---|
| Sunday | 7,8 and 14,15 |
| Monday | 4,5 and 11,12 |
| Tuesday | 1,2 and 8,9 |
| Wednesday | 5,6 and 12,13 |
| Thursday | 2,3 and 9,10 |
| Friday | 6,7 and 13,14 |
| Saturday | 3,4 and 10,11 |

| After Sunset: | |
|---|---|
| Sunday | 2,3 and 9,10 |
| Monday | 6,7 and 13,14 |
| Tuesday | 3,4 and 10,11 |
| Wednesday | 7,8 and 14,15 |
| Thursday | 4,5 and 11,12 |
| Friday | 1,2 and 8,9 |
| Saturday | 5,6 and 12,13 |

SPECIAL BONUS!

Twelve Zodiac Birth Certificates!

Dog's Astrological

# Birth Certificate

©Aquaruis Dog

## Aquarius Dog

**January 21-February 19**

**Symbol:** The Water Carrier. Aquarius – an Air Sign – belongs to the element which links all living beings – the life force that flows from the atmosphere through our bodies, and out into the atmosphere again.

**Key words:** Friendship, Eccentricity, and Freedom

**Dominant principle:** "I know" **Ruling Planet:** Saturn

**Stones:** Light Sapphire, Opal, Amethyst, and Garnet **Metal:** Tin **Lucky Days:** Wednesday, Saturday

**Special Advice:** Aquarius Dog is very creative and eager to learn. Aquarius might surprise you by demonstrating tricks you never taught him. He loves to impress other dogs with his stylish appearance. Don't scold him – this is just his way of showing how unique he is. He might feel depressed when deprived of companionship, whether human or animal. Aquarius is blessed with an inquisitive mind and is not afraid of technology. He may even program your remote control for you!

Your Dog's Photo Here

Dog's Name______________________________

Dog's Nickname______________________________

Dog's Date of Birth______________________________

KoZmoPets™

# Dog's Astrological Birth Certificate

©Pisces Dog

## Pisces Dog

### February 20-March 20

**Symbol:** Two fish joined together but pulling in opposite directions, exemplifying Pisces' dual and vacillating nature.

**Key words:** : Sensitive, Indecisive, Compassionate.

**Dominant principle:** "I believe" **Ruling Planet:** Jupiter

**Stones:** Sapphire, Moonstone **Metal:** Zinc **Lucky Days:** Monday, Thursday, Friday

**Special Advice:** Artistic and refined by nature, Pisces Dog has a strong aversion to unrefined speech. This dog also has a special flair for the theatrical, and loves to perform! Don't be surprised if your Pisces pet takes Hollywood by storm.

Your Dog's Photo Here

Dog's Name________________________

Dog's Nickname________________________

Dog's Date of Birth________________________

KoZmoPets™

# Dog's Astrological Birth Certificate

©Aries Dog

## Aries Dog

### March 21-April 20

**Symbol:** The Ram. Aries Dog is an aggressive leader, always ready to accept a challenge.
**Key words:** Enthusiasm, Pluck, Aggression
**Dominant principle:** "I am" **Ruling Planets:** Mars, Sun
**Stones:** Diamond, Ruby, Amethyst **Metals:** Iron, Steel **Lucky Days:** Tuesday, Sunday

**Special Advice:** Devoted Aries Dog takes your ailments and diseases upon himself. He remains tied to you in this way as long as there is a bond of affection. Don't be surprised if your guard dog feels uncomfortable in his own doghouse, since Aries is not a fan of confinement. Highly energetic, Aries Dog gets along best with an owner who is active and outgoing.

Your Dog's Photo Here

Dog's Name_______________________________

Dog's Nickname_______________________________

Dog's Date of Birth_______________________________

KoZmoPets™

## Dog's Astrological

# Birth Certificate

©Taurus Dog

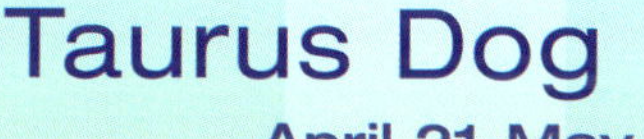

## Taurus Dog

### April 21-May 21

**Symbol:** The Bull. Like his symbol – a powerfully built, possessive animal – Taurus is unflinching in attack
**Key words:** Practicality, Possessiveness, Hedonism
**Dominant principle:** "I have" **Ruling Planets:** Venus, Moon
**Stones:** Sapphire, Agate, Turquoise, Nephrite **Metal:** Copper **Lucky Days:** Monday, Friday

**Special Advice:** Taurus Dog always shares your emotional unrest. He therefore does his doggy best to alleviate your problems and improve your relationships with other people. Taurus doesn't respond well to pressure and demanding people. Instead he prefers consistency and stability. Indecisive owners tend to confuse and unsettle Taurus Dog. Make good on all your promises to Taurus Dog, whether for outings, toys, or treats. If he waits too long for something he expects, he may think you have forgotten or changed your mind.

Your Dog's Photo Here

Dog's Name______________________________

Dog's Nickname______________________________

Dog's Date of Birth______________________________

# Dog's Astrological Birth Certificate

## Gemini Dog

**May 22-June 21**



**Symbol:** The Twins. Gemini Dog may display two very distinct personalities. This dual nature is reflected in his symbol, which resembles the Roman Numeral II.
**Key words:** Inventive, Studious, Active, Sly
**Dominant principle:** "I think" **Ruling Planet:** Mercury
**Stones:** Agate, Crystal, Garnet **Metals:** Gold, Silver **Lucky Days:** Wednesday, Sunday

**Special Advice:** Geminis loathe monotony and repetition. Your Gemini Dog loves to be entertained. Ever notice how much he enjoys watching TV and listening to music? Don't be a bore for Gemini Dog – who likes bright, easygoing and funny people. Feel free to sing even if you do not have the voice. Your pet will love it, especially if it is a top ten hit! Indulge Gemini's thirst for excitement by bringing your canine companion along on all sorts of expeditions.

Your Dog's Photo Here

Dog's Name______________________________

Dog's Nickname____________________________

Dog's Date of Birth__________________________

# Dog's Astrological Birth Certificate

©Cancer Dog

## Cancer Dog
### June 22-July 23

**Symbol:** The Crab. Like the sea creature that represents him, Cancer Dog has a soft, sensitive interior and a protective exterior shell.
**Key words:** Domestic, Security, Emotional, Support
**Dominant principle:** "I fool" **Ruling Planet:** Moon
**Stones:** Moonstone, Ruby, Emerald **Metal:** Silver **Lucky Days:** Monday, Thursday

**Special Advice:** Cancer Dog truly sees you, his human companion, as someone under his care. Very sensitive to the needs of elderly people and children, he intuitively knows when he's needed and never hesitates to offer help. Cancer Dog suffers anguish if his beloved family breaks up. He dislikes rude or noisy guests who intrude on the privacy of his human family. He may be injured when traveling with you.

Your Dog's Photo Here

Dog's Name______________________________

Dog's Nickname______________________________

Dog's Date of Birth______________________________

KoZmoPets™

## Dog's Astrological

# Birth Certificate

## Leo Dog

**July 24-August 23**



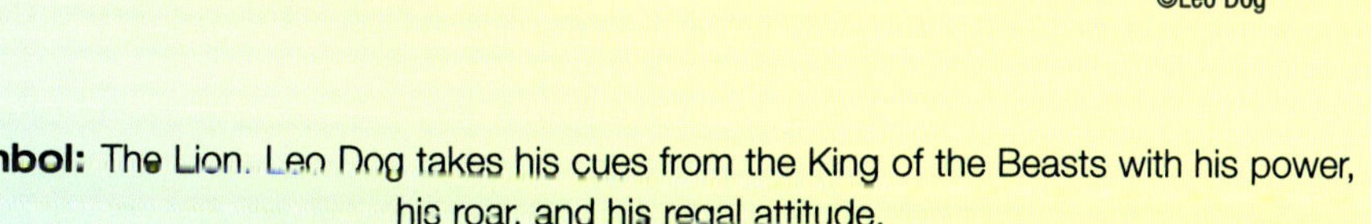

**Symbol:** The Lion. Leo Dog takes his cues from the King of the Beasts with his power, his roar, and his regal attitude.

**Key words:** Power, Generosity, Charisma

**Dominant principle:** "I will" **Ruling Planet:** Sun

**Stones:** Amber, Topaz, Emerald, Ruby, Onyx **Metal:** Gold **Lucky Day:** Sunday

**Special Advice:** Your Leo Dog may cause envious or jealous reactions in other people. Leo needs appreciation, and loves it when you openly enjoy his or her company. This dog loves any form of your affection, especially presents. Your Leo Dog repays you not only with all his love and loyalty, but also with many awards and prizes from top canine competitions!

Your Dog's Photo Here

Dog's Name______________________________

Dog's Nickname______________________________

Dog's Date of Birth______________________________

KoZmoPets™

# Dog's Astrological Birth Certificate

## Virgo Dog

### August 24-September 23

©Virgo Dog

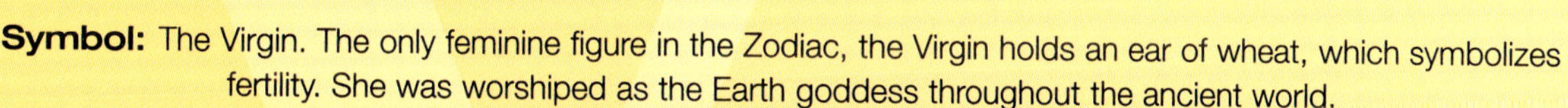

**Symbol:** The Virgin. The only feminine figure in the Zodiac, the Virgin holds an ear of wheat, which symbolizes fertility. She was worshiped as the Earth goddess throughout the ancient world.

**Key words:** Service, Practicality, Loyalty

**Dominant principle:** "I analyze" **Ruling Planet:** Mercury

**Stones:** Agate, Malachite, Carnelian, Topaz, Nephrite, and Yellow Sapphire

**Metals:** Copper, Tin **Lucky Day:** Wednesday

**Special Advice:** Virgo Dog is quite sensitive to unhealthy environments and to the ailments of other dogs. Thus it's important to protect him against harmful company. Invest total trust in your Virgo dog and he will protect you and your family and guard your home better than any security system.

Your Dog's Photo Here

Dog's Name______________________________

Dog's Nickname______________________________

Dog's Date of Birth______________________________

# Dog's Astrological Birth Certificate

©Libra Dog

## Libra Dog

### September 24-October 23

**Symbol:** The Scales. Libra's symbol is the only inanimate object among the Zodiac signs. Libras seek in others the balancing qualities they lack in themselves. This results in their frequent indecisiveness.

**Key words:** Cooperation, Companionship, Balance

**Dominant principle:** "I balance" **Ruling Planet:** Venus

**Stones:** Opal, Lazurite, Pearl, Chrysolite, Diamond **Lucky Days:** Friday, Saturday

**Special Advice:** A Libra dog is a dainty eater and requires a balanced diet. Because of Libra's curious nature, he or she is likely to fall into all kinds of traps. Make sure you don't accidentally shut Libra in your refrigerator! Libra Dog has a talent for mediating conflicts between people and will use his or her easy, elegant personality to release tension at home. Libra thrives in a bright and comfortable home environment. And especially loves an expensive haircut in a trendy salon!

Your Dog's Photo Here

Dog's Name______________________________

Dog's Nickname______________________________

Dog's Date of Birth______________________________

# Dog's Astrological Birth Certificate

## Scorpio Dog

### October 24–November 22



**Symbol:** The Scorpion and the Eagle. Together these animals rise above temptation. This sign is associated with both the life force and the life cycle
**Key words:** Tenacity, Rebirth, Mystery
**Dominant principle:** "I desire" **Ruling Planets:** Pluto, Mars
**Stones:** Ruby, Topaz, Aquamarine, Coral, Malachite **Metals:** Iron, Steel **Lucky Days:** Tuesday, Sunday

**Special Advice:** Scorpio Dog protects you in any situations. Very sensitive to aggressive instincts, he or she may have sudden angry outbursts. Scorpio can also bear a grudge. No matter what your emotions, never talk harshly to your Scorpio Dog and never force him or her to perform tricks for your guests if he does not want to. Scorpio Dog is an excellent tracer. He'll find, you know, that long lost sock of yours, the missing half of your favorite pair – and proudly deposit it in your lap!

Your Dog's Photo Here

Dog's Name______________________________

Dog's Nickname__________________________

Dog's Date of Birth________________________

## Sagittarius Dog

### November 23–December21



**Symbol:** The Centaur with the bow and arrow. Symbolic of the far-reaching, free-ranging, restless, and idealistic aims of the typical Sagittarian impulse
**Key words:** Liberty, Independence, Adventure **Dominant principle:** "I see"
**Ruling Planet:** Jupiter **Stones:** Topaz, Amethyst, Sapphire, Agate, Turquoise, Carbuncle, Emerald
**Metals:** Zinc, Tin **Lucky Day:** Thursday

**Special Advice:** Sagittarius Dog is somewhat touchy, often imagining insults, so be patient with him. To make him feel better, surround him with friends. He loves good company and showing off at parties! Sagittarius is a very lucky sign for race dogs. He also does well in exhibitions and competitions. While he is a marvel of neatness and order, this adventure-loving dog is always on the move. He might just join the astronauts on a moon walk if he had the chance!

Your Dog's Photo Here

Dog's Name____________________________

Dog's Nickname____________________________

Dog's Date of Birth____________________________

## Capricorn Dog

### December 22 –January 20

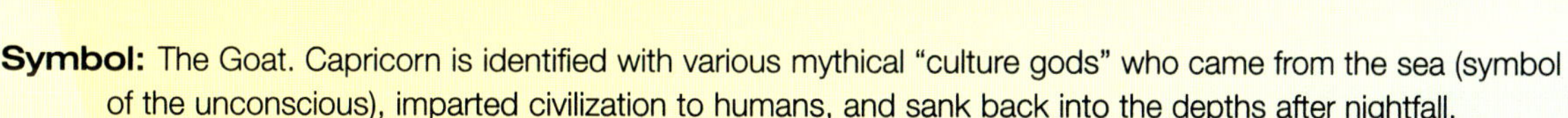

**Symbol:** The Goat. Capricorn is identified with various mythical "culture gods" who came from the sea (symbol of the unconscious), imparted civilization to humans, and sank back into the depths after nightfall.

**Key words:** Duty, Aspiration, and Ambition

**Dominant principle:** "I use" **Ruling Planets:** Saturn, Mars

**Stones:** Ruby, Onyx, Moonstone, Lazurite, Garnet **Metal:** Lead **Lucky Days:** Tuesday, Saturday

**Special Advice:** When well loved and cared for, Capricorn Dog may incite feelings of envy in your neighborhood – especially if you live in a competitive or showy area. Capricorn Dog offers you total devotion, and he or she wants you to show appreciation. If you are hosting a company party at your house, Capricorn Dog picks your boss out of the crowd like magic. If your boss is a dog person, canine Capricorn is sure to befriend him or her. Let your pet warm up your boss's heart – there's no better time to ask for that raise or promotion!

Your Dog's Photo Here

Dog's Name________________________________________

Dog's Nickname____________________________________

Dog's Date of Birth_________________________________

KoZmoPets™

# Notes

# Notes

# *Notes*

# Notes

# Notes

# Notes

# *Notes*

# Notes

# Notes

## *Notes*

# Notes

# Notes

## About the Author

Luba Matusovsky, a noted author/journalist/artist/art collector/inventor and – not least – pet lover, wrote Your Dog's Lifetime Horoscope because she wanted in an entertaining, informative way to help pet lovers better understand their pets and the role they play in each other's life.

A native of Moscow, Luba came to America from Russia to fulfill a promise to her father, and now lives in Denver with her husband, Edward. Other members of her family live in California.

She has many friends all over the world. She loves to travel and is a good cook. The founder of Pets Horoscopes, LLC, Luba is also the author of Your Cat's Lifetime Horoscope as a part of "KozmoPets" series line of greeting cards, posters, calendars, etc., portraying the same loveable, charming astro cats and dogs images found within her books.

Mrs. Matusovsky has a degree in economics, worked as a project coordinator at different international exhibitions and as a journalist for newspapers and magazines. She continues to pursue her interests in inventions (has a US patent for a household device), astrology, history, classical and jazz music. Your Dog's Lifetime Horoscope is Mrs. Matusovsky's first book to be published in the USA.

Your Dog's Lifetime Horoscope
By Luba Matusovsky
2nd edition
Cover and book design: Vladimir Sonkin
Illustrator: Oleg Urlov
Editor: Ron Kenner
ISBN-10: 0-98268-341-3
ISBN-13: 978-0-9826834-1-5
$17.95 (CAN $19.95)
Pets Horoscopes, LLC (2010)


lm@petshoroscopes.com



Published in 2010 by Pets Horoscopes, LLC
www.kozmopets.com
Printed in China